Beef Air Fryer Cookbook

Quick & Easy, Extra Crispy Recipes to Bake, Fry, Grill and Roast the Most Loved American Dishes.
The Secrets for Air Frying Like a Pro

Chef Max Wilbur

Table of Contents

INTRODUCTION

The Air Fryer Oven Grill is the perfect addition to any kitchen. It's a modern and stylish countertop cooking appliance that cooks faster and more efficiently than your standard electric or gas grill. It can be used on its own as a small griller or in conjunction with your larger countertop oven as an air fryer.

The Air Fryer has a unique design that allows you to cook a wide range of foods that your traditional stovetop or electric grills cannot handle. The large handle and spacious cooking area make it an attractive choice for anyone who wants to save time and space in your kitchen.

Step By Step Directions to Use the Air Fryer Grill

Step one:

Preheat the air fryer, add desired foods to the basket and close the lid. Turn the vent control knob to the "AIR DRY" position. Set the timer to cook for 20 minutes at 400°F (200°C). To use as a crockpot, set on low heat and cook for 8 hours or overnight.

Step two:

Remove food from the basket, drain excess oil, and serve. You may also season or marinate for further flavor enhancement before cooking (optional).

After cooking, keep calm in a covered container until ready to eat.

For best results, does not freeze or store in the refrigerator for longer than three days (if possible), as this will remove some of the oils from foods.

If you must store longer, at a low temperature (50 – 60 and use within 2-4 days. You may also season or marinate for further flavor enhancement before cooking (optional).

Tips and Tricks for Using the Air Fryer Grill

Use fresh ingredients that produce less moisture - consider no-oil salads or sautéed vegetables instead of fried.

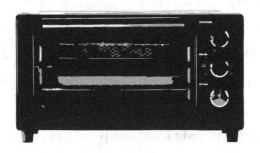

Care and maintenance

For best results, never immerse or submerge air fryer in water or any other liquid during use. Avoid letting water get on the heating element or fan, as this can cause damage to these parts and may affect their performance over time. There are no moving parts that will deteriorate over time; therefore, cleaning all removable parts will only require that they be wiped clean with a damp cloth. Use the only high-quality non-abrasive mild cleaner on non-removable components such as the door gasket or drip tray, as this can affect their performance. Use only silicone-based lubricants for cleaning your air fryer grill; do not use aerosol sprays in this area as these can damage delicate internal components. Avoid touching metal surfaces inside the appliance with your hands, as this can result in skin rashes or other issues

Use only mild dish detergent and hot water on a soft sponge to improve the longevity of the machine's finish.

It can cook up to 10 pounds of food in just 8 minutes!

The device cooks food by circulating air around the food. In just 30 minutes, you can have a delicious meal like never before. There are no dirty pans to clean and no wasted oil, making this device a win-win for both your health and your budget.

It is a tool that will revolutionize the way you cook. Unbox, prepare and start cooking.

The air fryer grill is easy to use, with the LCD panel on its side shows you the time and temperature settings. You can set up 8 different modes to cook your favorite foods. If you only want 2 minutes per side, use that mode; if you prefer 4 minutes per side, use that mode; if you wish to 6 minutes cooking time per side, then use the extended cooking mode.

Its 4 heat settings make sure your food doesn't burn before cooking is completed. It also has a power outlet to plug in your device and keep it safe from electricity spikes or power surges during those hot summer days. The food inside the air fryer cannot burn because of the non-stick pan plates used to make sure no oil gets on the food as you are cooking.

It also has a cool-touch exterior so that kids can use this without worry about burning their hands on the hot pan surface. The glass lid can be opened after it has been cooked so you can serve it in a bowl or plate without having to wait for the cool-down of the unit before serving.

This device is similar to other air fryers, except for how much air it can maintain at a time. This allows for more consistent cooking and better results every time.

With your Air Fryer Grill, you can prepare meals faster than ever before. You can use almost any cooking utensil to fry, bake, roast, broil, and much more. You can create gourmet meals in a fraction of the time it takes with traditional grill cookbooks or no cookers'

This product can be used for just about any type of food you can think of, so long as you are willing to try something new. It is easy to use and easy to clean, and uniquely can be used in the oven or on your grill or stovetop. The versatility will make you think about this tool more often than it took you to learn how great it is!!

Air Fryer Cooking Times

	Temp (°F)	Time (min)		Temp (°F)	Time (min)
Vegetables					
Asparagus (sliced 1-inch)	400°F	5	**Onions** (peart)	400°F	10
Beets (whole)	400°F	40	**Parsnips**	380°F	15
Broccoli (florets)	400°F	6	**Peppers** (1-inch chunks)	400°F	15
Brussels Sprouts (halved)	380°F	15	**Potatoes** (small baby, 1.5 lbs)	400°F	15
Carrots (sliced 1/2-inch)	380°F	15	**Potatoes** (1-inch chunks)	400°F	12
Cauliflower (florets)	400°F	12	**Potatoes** (baked whole)	400°F	40
Com on the cob	390°F	6	**Squash** (1/2-inch chunks)	400°F	12
Eggplant (11/2-inch cubes)	400°F	15	**Sweet Potato**	380°F	30 to 35
Fennel (quartered)	370°F	15	**Tomatoes** (cherry)	400°F	4
Green Beans	400°F	5	**Tomatoes** (halves)	350°F	10
Kale leaves	250°F	12	**Zucchini** (1/2-inch sticks)	400°F	12
Mushrooms (sliced 1/4-inch)	400°F	5			

Chicken

Breasts, bone in (1.25 lbs.)	370°F	25	Legs, bone in (1.75 lbs.)	380°F	30
Breasts, boneless (4 oz.)	380°F	12	Wings (2 lbs.)	400°F	12
Drumsticks (2.5 lbs.)	370°F	20	Game Hen (halved - 2 lbs.)	390°F	20
Thighs, bone In (2 lbs.)	380°F	22	Whole Chicken (6.5 lbs.)	360°F	75
Thighs, boneless (1.5 lbs.)	380°F	18 to 20	Tenders	360°F	8 to 10

Beef

Burger (4 oz.)	370°F	16 to 20	Meatballs (3-inch)	380°F	10
Filet Mignon (8 oz.)	400°F	18	Ribeye, bone In (1-inch, 8 oz.)	400°F	10 to 15
Flank Steak (1.5 lbs.)	400°F	12	Sirloin steaks (1-inch, 12 oz.)	400°F	9 to 14
London Broil (2 lbs.)	400°F	20 to 28	Beef Eye Round Roast (4 lbs.)	390°F	45 to 55
Meatballs (1-inch)	380°F	7			

Pork and Lamb

Loin (2 lbs.)	360°F	55	Bacon (thick cut)	400°F	6 to 10

Pork Chops, bone in (1-inch, 6.5 oz.)	400°F	12	**Sausages**	380°F	15
Tenderloin (1 lb.)	370°F	15	**Lamb Loin Chops** (1-	400° F	8 to 12
Bacon (regular)	400°F	5 to 7	**Rack of lamb** (1.5 - 2 lbs.)	380°F	22
Fish and Seafood					
Calamari (8 oz.)	400°F	4	**Tuna steak**	400°F	7 to 10
Fish Fillet (1-inch, 8oz.)	400°F	10	**Scallops**	400°F	5 to 7
Salmon, fillet (6oz.)	380°F	12	**Shrimp**	400°F	5
Swordfish steak	400°F	10			
Frozen Foods					
Onion Rings (12 oz.)	400°F	8	**Fish Sticks** (10 oz.)	400°F	10
Thin French Fries (20 oz.)	400°F	14	**Fish Fillets** (1/2-inch, 10	400°F	14
Thick French Fries (17 oz.)	400°F	18	**Chicken Nuggets** (12	400°F	10
Mozzarella Sticks (11 oz.)	400°F	8	**Breaded Shrimp**	400°F	9
Pot Stickers (10 oz.)	400°F	8			

Caraway Crusted Beef Steaks

Preparation time: 5 minutes

Cooking time: 10 minutes

Serving: 4

Ingredients:

- 4 beef steaks
- 2 teaspoons caraway seeds
- 2 teaspoons garlic powder
- Sea salt and cayenne pepper, to taste
- 1 tablespoon melted butter
- 1/3 cup almond flour
- 2 eggs, beaten

Directions:

- Attach the beef steaks to a large bowl and toss with the caraway seeds, garlic powder, and salt and pepper until well coated.
- Merge together the melted butter and almond flour in a bowl. Pour the eggs in a different bowl.
- Set the seasoned steaks in the eggs, then dip in the almond and butter mixture.
- Arrange the coated steaks in the air fry basket.
- Select Air Fry, Super Convection. Set temperature to 355F (179C) and set time to 10 minutes. Press Start/Stop to begin preheating.
- Once preheated, place the basket on the air fry position. Set the steaks once halfway through to ensure even cooking.
- When cooking is processed, the internal temperature of the beef steaks should reach at least 145F (63C) on a meat thermometer.
- Set the steaks to plates. Let cool and serve hot.

Nutrition: Calories: 327 Fat: 18g Protein: 34g

Mushroom in Bacon-Wrapped fillets Mignons

Preparation time: 10 minutes

Cooking time: 13 minutes

Serving: 8

Ingredients:

- 1 ounce (28 g) dried porcini mushrooms
- 1/2 teaspoon granulated white sugar
- 1/2 teaspoon salt
- 1/2 teaspoon ground white pepper
- 8 (4-ounce / 113-g) fillets mignons or beef tenderloin steaks
- 8 thin-cut bacon strips

Directions:

- Put the mushrooms, sugar, salt, and white pepper in a spice grinder and grind to combine.
- On a clean work surface, rub the fillets mignons with the mushroom mixture, then wrap each filet with a bacon strip. Secure with toothpicks if necessary.
- Arrange the bacon-wrapped fillets mignons in the air fry basket, seam side down.
- Select Air Fry, Super Convection. Set temperature to 400°F (205°C) and set time to 13 minutes. Press Start/Stop to begin preheating.

- Once preheated, place the basket on the air fry position. Flip the fillets halfway through.
- When cooking is complete, the fillets should be medium rare.
- Serve immediately.

Nutrition: Calories: 351 Fat: 15g Protein: 56g

Air Fried Beef and Mushroom Stroganoff

Preparation time: 15 minutes

Cooking time: 14 minutes

Serving: 4

Ingredients:

- 1-pound (454 g) beef steak, thinly sliced
- 8 ounces (227 g) mushrooms, sliced
- 1 whole onion, chopped
- 2 cups beef broth
- 1 cup sour cream
- 4 tablespoons butter, melted
- 2 cups cooked egg noodles

Directions:

- Merge the mushrooms, onion, beef broth, sour cream and butter in a bowl until well blended. Add the beef steak to another bowl.
- Scatter the mushroom mixture over the steak and let marinate for 10 minutes.
- Whisk the marinated steak in a baking pan.
- Select Bake, Super Convection, set temperature to 400F (205C) and set time to 14 minutes. Press Start/Stop to begin preheating.
- Once preheated, place the pan on the bake position. Set the steak halfway through the cooking time.
- When cooking is processed, the steak should be browned and the vegetables should be tender.
- Serve hot with the cooked egg noodles.

Nutrition: Calories: 361 Fat: 17g Protein: 42g Carbs: 2 g

Cinnamon-Beef Kofta

Preparation time: 10 minutes

Cooking time: 13 minutes

Serving: 6

Ingredients:

- 11/2 pounds (680 g) lean ground beef
- 1 teaspoon onion powder
- 1/3 teaspoon ground cinnamon
- 1/3 teaspoon ground dried turmeric
- 1 teaspoon ground cumin
- 1/3 teaspoon salt
- 1/4 teaspoon cayenne
- 12 (31/2- to 4-inch-long) cinnamon sticks
- Cooking spray

Directions:

- Spritz the air fry basket with cooking spray.

- Merge all the ingredients, except for the cinnamon sticks, in a large bowl. Toss to mix well.
- Divide and shape the mixture into 12 balls then wrap each ball around each cinnamon stick and leave a quarter of the length uncovered.
- Arrange the beef-cinnamon sticks in the prepared basket and spritz with cooking spray.
- Select Air Fry, Super Convection. Set temperature to 375F (190C) and set time to 13 minutes. Press Start/Stop to begin preheating.
- Once preheated, place the basket on the air fry position. Flip the sticks halfway through the cooking.
- When cooking is processed, the beef should be browned.
- Serve immediately.

Nutrition: Calories: 342 Fat: 12g Protein: 42g Carbs: 1 g

Reuben Beef Rolls with Thousand Island Sauce

Preparation time: 15 minutes

Cooking time: 10 minutes

Serving: 5

Ingredients:

- 1/2 pound (227 g) cooked corned beef, chopped
- 1/2 cup drained and chopped sauerkraut
- 1 (8-ounce / 227-g) package cream cheese, softened
- 1/2 cup shredded Swiss cheese
- 20 slices prosciutto
- Cooking spray
- Thousand Island Sauce:
- 1/4 cup chopped dill pickles

- 1/4 cup tomato sauce
- 1/3 cup mayonnaise
- Fresh thyme leaves, for garnish
- 2 tablespoons sugar
- 1/8 teaspoon fine sea salt
- Ground black pepper, to taste

Directions:
- Spritz the air fry basket with cooking spray.
- Combine the beef, sauerkraut, cream cheese, and Swiss cheese in a large bowl. Stir to mix well.
- Unroll a slice of prosciutto on a clean work surface, and then top with another slice of prosciutto crosswise. Scoop up 4 tablespoons of the beef mixture in the center.
- Fold the top slice sides over the filling as the ends of the roll, then roll up the long sides of the bottom prosciutto and make it into a roll shape. Overlap the sides by about 1 inch. Repeat with remaining filling and prosciutto.
- Arrange the rolls in the prepared basket, seam side down, and spritz with cooking spray.
- Select Air Fry, Super Convection. Set temperature to 400F (205C) and set time to 10 minutes. Press Start/Stop to begin preheating.
- Once preheated, place the basket on the air fry position. Flip the rolls halfway through.

- When cooking is complete, the rolls should be golden and crispy.
- Meanwhile, merge the ingredients for the sauce in a small bowl. Stir to mix well.
- Serve the rolls with the dipping sauce.

Nutrition: Calories: 328 Fat: 19g Protein: 46g Carbs: 1.2 g

Salsa Beef Meatballs

Preparation time: 10 minutes

Cooking time: 10 minutes

Serving: 4

Ingredients:

- 1-pound (454 g) ground beef (85% lean)
- 1/2 cup salsa
- 1/4 cup red bell peppers
- 1 large egg, beaten
- 1/4 cup chopped onions
- 1/2 teaspoon chili powder
- 1 clove garlic, minced
- 1/2 teaspoon ground cumin
- 1 teaspoon fine sea salt

- Lime wedges, for serving
- Cooking spray

Directions:

- Spritz the air fry basket with cooking spray.
- Merge all the ingredients in a large bowl. Stir to mix well.
- Divide and shape the mixture into 1-inch balls. Arrange the balls in the basket and spritz with cooking spray.
- Select Air Fry, Super Convection. Set temperature to 350°F (180°C) and set time to 10 minutes. Press Start/Stop to begin preheating.
- Once preheated, place the basket on the air fry position. Flip the balls with tongs halfway through.
- When cooking is complete, the balls should be well browned.
- Transfer the balls on a plate and squeeze the lime wedges over before serving.

Nutrition: Calories: 348 Fat: 19g Protein: 46g Carbs: 2.1 g

Simple Ground Beef with Zucchini

Preparation time: 5 minutes

Cooking time: 12 minutes

Serving: 4

Ingredients:

- 11/2 pounds (680 g) ground beef
- 1 pound (454 g) chopped zucchini
- 2 tablespoons extra-virgin olive oil
- 1 teaspoon dried oregano
- 1 teaspoon dried basil
- 1 teaspoon dried rosemary
- 2 tablespoons fresh chives, chopped

Directions:

- In a large bowl, merge all the ingredients, except for the chives, until well blended.
- Place the beef and zucchini mixture in the baking pan.
- Select Bake, Super Convection, set temperature to 400°F (205°C) and set time to 12 minutes. Press Start/Stop to begin preheating.
- Once preheated, place the pan on the bake position.
- When cooking is processed, the beef should be browned and the zucchini should be tender.
- Divide the beef and zucchini mixture among four serving dishes. Top with fresh chives and serve hot.

Nutrition: Calories: 311 Fat: 20g Protein: 41g Carbs: 3.1 g

Sumptuous Beef and Pork Sausage Meatloaf

Preparation time: 10 minutes

Cooking time: 25 minutes

Serving: 4

Ingredients:

- 1/3 pound (340 g) ground chuck
- 4 ounces (113 g) ground pork sausage
- 2 eggs, beaten
- 1 cup Parmesan cheese, grated
- 1 cup chopped shallot
- 3 tablespoons plain milk
- 1 tablespoon oyster sauce
- 1 tablespoon fresh parsley

- 1 teaspoon garlic paste
- 1 teaspoon chopped porcini mushrooms
- 1/2 teaspoon cumin powder
- Seasoned salt and crushed red pepper flakes, to taste

Directions:

- In a large bowl, merge all the ingredients until well blended.
- Place the meat mixture in the baking pan. Use a spatula to press the mixture to fill the pan.
- Select Bake, Super Convection, set temperature to 360F (182C) and set time to 25 minutes. Press Start/Stop to begin preheating.
- Once preheated, place the pan on the bake position.
- When cooking is complete, the meatloaf should be well browned.
- Let the meatloaf rest for 5 minutes. Transfer to a serving dish and slice. Serve warm.

Nutrition: Calories: 317 Fat: 23g Protein: 46g Carbs: 1.2 g

Lahmacun (Turkish Pizza)

Preparation time: 20 minutes

Cooking time: 10 minutes

Serving: 4

Ingredients:

- 4 (6-inch) flour tortillas

For the Meat Topping:

- 4 ounces (113 g) ground lamb or 85% lean ground beef
- 1/4 cup chopped green bell pepper
- 1/4 cup chopped fresh parsley
- 1 small plum tomato, deseeded and chopped
- 2 tablespoons chopped yellow onion
- 1 garlic clove, minced
- 2 teaspoons tomato paste
- 1/4 teaspoon sweet paprika

- 1/4 teaspoon ground cumin

- 1/4 teaspoon red pepper flakes

- 1/8 teaspoon ground allspice

- 1/8 teaspoon kosher salt

- 1/8 teaspoon black pepper

For Serving:

- 1/4 cup chopped fresh mint

- 1 teaspoon extra-virgin olive oil

- 1 lemon, cut into wedges

Directions:

- Combine all the ingredients for the meat topping in a medium bowl until well mixed.

- Lay the tortillas on a clean work surface. Spoon the meat mixture on the tortillas and spread all over.

- Place the tortillas in the air fry basket.

- Select Air Fry, Super Convection. Set temperature to 400°F (205°C) and set time to 10 minutes. Press Start/Stop to begin preheating.

- Once preheated, place the basket on the air fry position.

- When cooking is complete, the edge of the tortilla should be golden and the meat should be lightly browned.

- Transfer them to a serving dish. Top with chopped fresh mint and drizzle with olive oil. Squeeze the lemon wedges on top and serve.

Nutrition: Calories: 313 Fat: 27g Protein: 31g Carbs: 2.1 g

Thai Curry Beef Meatballs

Preparation time: 5 minutes

Cooking time: 15 minutes

Serving: 4

Ingredients:

- 1-pound (454 g) ground beef
- 1 tablespoon sesame oil
- 2 teaspoons chopped lemongrass
- 1 teaspoon red Thai curry paste
- 1 teaspoon Thai seasoning blend
- Juice and zest of 1/2 lime
- Cooking spray

Directions:

- Spritz the air fry basket with cooking spray.

- In a medium bowl, merge all the ingredients until well blended.
- Shape the meat mixture into 24 meatballs and arrange them in the basket.
- Select Air Fry, Super Convection. Set temperature to 380F (193C) and set time to 15 minutes. Press Start/Stop to begin preheating.
- Once preheated, place the basket on the air fry position. Flip the meatballs.
- When cooking is processed, the meatballs should be browned.
- Transfer the meatballs to plates. Let cool for 5 minutes before serving.

Nutrition: Calories: 338 Fat: 29g Protein: 56g Carbs: 3, 1

Stuffed Beef Tenderloin with Feta Cheese

Preparation time: 10 minutes

Cooking time: 10 minutes

Serving: 4

Ingredients:

- 11/2 pounds (680 g) beef tenderloin, pounded to 1/4 inch thick
- 3 teaspoons sea salt
- 1 teaspoon ground black pepper
- 2 ounces (57 g) creamy goat cheese
- 1/2 cup crumbled feta cheese
- 1/4 cup finely chopped onions
- 2 cloves garlic, minced
- Cooking spray

Directions:

- Spritz the air fry basket with cooking spray.

- Unfold the beef tenderloin on a clean work surface. Rub the salt and pepper all over the beef tenderloin to season.
- Make the filling for the stuffed beef tenderloins: Combine the goat cheese, feta, onions, and garlic in a medium bowl. Stir until well blended.
- Spoon the mixture in the center of the tenderloin. Roll the tenderloin up tightly like rolling a burrito and use some kitchen twine to tie the tenderloin.
- Arrange the tenderloin in the air fry basket.
- Select Air Fry, Super Convection. Set temperature to 400F (205C) and set time to 10 minutes. Press Start/Stop to begin preheating.
- Once preheated, place the basket on the air fry position. Flip the tenderloin halfway through.
- When cooking is complete, the instant-read thermometer inserted in the center of the tenderloin should register 135F (57C) for medium-rare.
- Transfer to a platter and serve immediately.

Nutrition: Calories: 321 Fat: 11g Protein: 30g Carbs: 1.9 g

Teriyaki Beef Short Ribs with Pomegranate

Preparation time: 15 minutes

Cooking time: 1 hour

Serving: 4 to 6

Ingredients:

- 1 cup tamari soy sauce or dark soy sauce
- 1/2 cup packed brown sugar
- 1/4 cup pomegranate molasses
- 2 or 3 scallions, finely chopped (both white and green parts)
- 4 cloves garlic, minced
- 1 tablespoon oyster sauce
- 2 teaspoons Worcestershire sauce
- 2 teaspoons mirin
- 1 teaspoon vegetable oil

- 1 teaspoon grated fresh ginger
- 1 teaspoon Asian chili sauce
- 6 beef short ribs, 31/2 to 4 inches long and 2 inches thick
- Chopped scallion, for garnish
- 1/3 cup pomegranate seeds, for garnish

Directions:

- Merge the marinade ingredients in a saucepan and simmer over medium heat for 3 to 5 minutes, until the sugar has dissolved, stirring occasionally. Remove from the heat and let the mixture cool for 30 minutes. Divide the marinade into two equal portions. Store one half in the refrigerator for basting. Use the remaining half as the marinade.

- Trim off any excess fat or straggling meat from the surface of the ribs. Do not attempt to remove any internal fat. Place the ribs in a resalable plastic bag and add the marinade. Using tongs, gently turn the ribs to coat. Secure the bag and place in the refrigerator for 6 to 12 hours.

- Prepare the grill for medium heat with indirect cooking.

- Set a tumble basket on a large cutting board. This will keep your floors and countertop clean. Remove the ribs from the bag and place them in the basket. Discard any marinade left in the bag. Secure the basket.

- Place the basket on the preheated grill with a drip pan underneath, making sure that it doesn't get in the way of the basket as it turns. Cook for 1 to 11/2 hours, or until the ribs have rendered the majority of their fat and have reached an internal temperature of 170F (77C) to 180F (82C).
- Heat the reserved marinade in a bowl in the microwave for 1 minute. Stir. Begin basting with this mixture during the last 20 to 30 minutes of cooking time.
- Remove the basket from the grill and place on a heat-resistant cutting board. Let the ribs rest for 5 minutes or so. Carefully open the basket and plate the ribs. Serve garnished with the chopped scallion and pomegranate seeds.

Nutrition: Calories: 333 Fat: 23g Protein: 32g Carbs: 3 g.

Prime Beef Rib Roast

Preparation time: 10 minutes

Cooking time: 2 hours

Serving: 2

Ingredients:

- 1 (12 pound / 5.4-kg) bone-in beef rib roast (a four-bone roast)
- 3 tablespoons salt
- 1 1/2 tablespoons ground black pepper
- Horseradish sauce
- 1/2 cup sour cream
- 1/4 cup prepared horseradish
- 2 tablespoons Dijon mustard
- Fist sized chunk of smoking wood (or 1 cup wood chips)

Directions:

- Flavor the rib roast with the salt and pepper. Fridge for at least two hours, preferably overnight.
- One hour before cooking, detach the rib roast from the refrigerator. Truss the roast, and then skewer it on the rotisserie spit, securing it with the spit forks. Let the beef rest until the grill is pre-heated. Submerge the smoking wood in water and let it soak until the grill is ready.
- Set the grill up for medium-high heat.

- Set the spit on the grill, Add the smoking wood to the fire, close the lid, and cook the beef until it reaches 120F (49C) in its thickest part for medium-rare, about 2 hours. (Cook to 115F (46C) for rare, 130F (54C) for medium.)
- Detach the rib roast from the rotisserie spit and remove the twine trussing the roast. Be careful - the spit and forks are blazing hot. Let the beef rest, and while the beef is resting, whisk together the ingredients for the horseradish sauce. To carve the beef, cut the bones off of the roast, then slice the roast and serve.

Nutrition: Calories: 368 Fat: 16g Protein: 26g Carbs: 3.1 g

Beef Jerky

Preparation Time: 15 minutes

Cooking Time: 3 hours

Servings: 4

Ingredients:

- 11/2 pounds beef round, trimmed
- 1/2 cup Worcestershire sauce
- 1/2 cup low-sodium soy sauce
- 2 teaspoons honey
- 1 teaspoon liquid smoke
- 2 teaspoons onion powder
- 1/2 teaspoon red pepper flakes
- Ground black pepper, as required

Directions:

- In a zip-top bag, place the beef and freeze for 1-2 hours to firm up.
- Bring the meat onto a cutting board and cut against the grain into 1/8-¼-inch strips.

- In a large bowl, add the remaining ingredients and mix until well combined.
- Add the steak slices and coat with the mixture generously.
- Refrigerate to marinate for about 4-6 hours.
- Remove the beef slices from bowl and with paper towels, pat dry them.
- Divide the steak strips onto the cooking trays and arrange in an even layer.
- Select "Dehydrate" and then adjust the temperature to 160 degrees F.
- Set the timer for 3 hours and press the "Start".
- When the display shows "Add Food" inserts 1 tray in the top position and another in the center position.
- After 11/2 hours, switch the position of cooking trays.
- Meanwhile, in a small pan, add the remaining ingredients over medium heat and cook for about 10 minutes, stirring occasionally.
- When cooking time is complete, remove the trays from Vortex.

Nutrition: Calories 372   Total Fat 10.7 g   Saturated Fat 4 g   Cholesterol 152 mg Sodium 2000 mg   Total Carbs 12 g   Fiber 0.2 g   Sugar 11.3 g   Protein 53.8 g

Beef Fillet with Garlic Mayo

Preparation Time: 10 Minutes

Cooking Time: 40 Minutes

Servings: 8

Ingredients:

- 3 lb. beef fillet
- 1 cup mayonnaise
- 4 tbsp. Dijon mustard
- 1/3 cup sour cream
- 1/4 cup chopped tarragon
- 2 tbsp. chopped chives
- 2 cloves garlic (minced)
- Salt and black pepper, to taste

Directions:

- Preheat the air fryer to 370F.

- Season beef using salt and pepper, transfer to the air fryer, and cook for 20 minutes. Remove and set aside.
- In a bowl, whisk the mustard and tarragon. Add the beef and toss, return to the air fryer and cook for 20 minutes.
- In a separate bowl, mix the garlic, sour cream, mayonnaise, chives, salt, and pepper. Whisk and set aside.
- Serve the beef with the garlic-mayo spread.

Nutrition: Calories: 400kcal, Fat: 12g, Carb: 26g, Proteins: 19g

Montreal Steak

Preparation Time: 5 minutes

Cooking Time: 7 minutes

Servings: 2

Ingredients:

- 12 oz. steak
- 1/2 tsp. liquid smoke
- 1 tbsp. soy sauce
- 1/2 tbsp. cocoa powder
- 1 tbsp. Montreal steak seasoning
- Pepper
- Salt

Directions:

- Add steak, liquid smoke, soy sauce, and steak seasonings into the large zip-lock bag. Coat well and place in the refrigerator for overnight.
- Spray air fryer basket with cooking spray.
- Place marinated steaks into the air fryer
- Cook at 375 F for 7 minutes. Turn after 5 minutes to another side.
- Serve and enjoy.

Nutrition: Calories 355 Fat 9 g Carbohydrates 1 g Sugar 0.3 g Protein 62 g Cholesterol 80 mg

Garlic Pork Chops

Preparation Time: 5 minutes

Cooking Time: 20 minutes

Servings: 5

Ingredients:

- 2 lbs. pork chops
- 2 tbsp. garlic, minced
- 1 tbsp. fresh parsley
- 2 tbsp. olive oil
- 2 tbsp. fresh lemon juice
- Pepper
- Salt

Directions:

- In a small bowl, merge together garlic, parsley, oil, and lemon juice.
- Season pork chops with pepper and salt.
- Rub garlic mixture over the pork chops and allow to marinate for 30 minutes.
- Add marinated pork chops into the air fryer and cook at 400 F for 10 minutes.
- Turn pork chops to another side and cook for 10 minutes more.
- Serve and enjoy.

Nutrition: Calories 625 Fat 50 g Carbohydrates 2 g Sugar 0.5 g Protein 40 g Cholesterol 124 mg

Cheese Herb Pork Chops

Preparation Time: 5 minutes

Cooking Time: 9 minutes

Servings: 2

Ingredients:

- 2 pork chops, boneless
- 1 tsp. herb de Provence
- 1 tsp. paprika
- 4 tbsp. parmesan cheese, grated
- 1/3 cup almond flour
- 1/2 tsp. Cajun seasoning

Directions:

- Preheat the air fryer to 350 F.
- Mix together almond flour, Cajun seasoning, herb de Provence, paprika, and cheese.
- Spray pork chops with cooking spray and coat pork chops with almond flour mixture and place into the air fryer basket.
- Cook for 9 minutes.
- Serve and enjoy.

Nutrition: Calories 340 Fat 26 g Carbohydrates 2 g Sugar 0.5 g Protein 24 g Cholesterol 124 mg

Creole Pork Chops

Preparation Time: 10 minutes

Cooking Time: 12 minutes

Servings: 6

Ingredients:

- 1 1/2 lbs. pork chops, boneless
- 1 tsp. garlic powder
- 5 tbsp. parmesan cheese, grated
- 1/3 cup almond flour
- 1 1/2 tsp. paprika
- 1 tsp. Creole seasoning

Directions:

- Preheat the air fryer to 360 F.
- Add all ingredients except pork chops into the zip-lock bag. Mix well.
- Add pork chops into the bag. Seal bag and shake until well coated.
- Spray air fryer basket with cooking spray.
- Place pork chops into the air fryer basket and cook for 12 minutes.
- Serve and enjoy.

Nutrition: Calories 400 Fat 31 g Carbohydrates 1 g Sugar 0.4 g Protein 28 g Cholesterol 243 mg

Jerk Pork

Preparation Time: 10 minutes

Cooking Time: 20 minutes

Servings: 4

Ingredients:

- 1 1/2 lbs. pork butt, chopped into pieces
- 3 tbsp. jerk paste

Directions:

- Add meat and jerk paste into the bowl and coat well. Place in the fridge for overnight.
- Spray air fryer basket with cooking spray.
- Preheat the air fryer to 390 F.
- Add marinated meat into the air fryer and cook for 20 minutes. Turn halfway through.
- Serve and enjoy.

Nutrition: Calories 325 Fat 12 g Carbohydrates 0.5 g Sugar 0 g Protein 52 g Cholesterol 124 mg

Cumin Lamb

Preparation Time: 10 minutes

Cooking Time: 10 minutes

Servings: 4

Ingredients:

- 1 lb. lamb, cut into 2-inch pieces
- 1/4 tsp. liquid stevia
- 2 tbsp. olive oil
- 1/2 tsp. cayenne
- 2 tbsp. ground cumin
- 2 red chili peppers, chopped
- 1 tbsp. garlic, minced
- 1 tbsp. soy sauce
- 1 tsp. salt

Directions:

- In a small bowl, mix together cumin and cayenne.
- Rub meat with cumin mixture and place in a large bowl.
- Add oil, soy sauce, garlic, chili peppers, stevia, and salt over the meat. Coat well and place in the refrigerator for overnight.
- Add marinated meat to the air fryer and cook at 360 F for 10 minutes.
- Serve and enjoy.

Nutrition: Calories 285 Fat 16 g Carbohydrates 2 g Sugar 0.5 g Protein 33 g Cholesterol 123 mg

Juicy and Tender Steak

Preparation Time: 10 minutes

Cooking Time: 12 minutes

Servings: 2

Ingredients:

- 2 rib-eye steak
- 3 tbsp. fresh parsley, chopped
- 1 stick butter, softened
- 1 1/2 tsp. Worcestershire sauce
- 3 garlic cloves, minced
- Pepper
- Salt

Directions:

- In a bowl, merge together butter, Worcestershire sauce, garlic, parsley, and salt and place in the refrigerator.
- Preheat the air fryer to 400 F.
- Season steak with pepper and salt.
- Place seasoned steak in the air fryer and cook for 12 minutes. Turn halfway through.
- Remove steak from air fryer and top with butter mixture.
- Serve and enjoy.

Nutrition: Calories 590 Fat 57 g Carbohydrates 3 g Sugar 0.5 g Protein 16 g Cholesterol 423 mg

Rosemary Beef Roast

Preparation Time: 10 minutes

Cooking Time: 45 minutes

Servings: 6

Ingredients:

- 2 lbs. beef roast
- 1 tbsp. olive oil
- 1 tsp. rosemary
- 1 tsp. thyme
- 1/4 tsp. pepper
- 1 tsp. salt

Directions:

- Preheat the air fryer to 360 F.
- Mix together oil, rosemary, thyme, pepper, and salt and rub over the meat.
- Place meat in the air fryer and cook for 45 minutes.
- Serve and enjoy.

Nutrition: Calories 300 Fat 12 g Carbohydrates 0.5 g Sugar 0 g Protein 46 g Cholesterol 123 mg

Air Fried Steak

Preparation Time: 10 minutes

Cooking Time: 10 minutes

Servings: 2

Ingredients:

- 2 sirloin steaks
- 2 tsp. olive oil
- 2 tbsp. steak seasoning
- Pepper
- Salt

Directions:

- Preheat the air fryer to 350 F.
- Set steak with olive oil and season with steak seasoning, pepper, and salt.
- Spray air fryer basket with cooking spray and place steak in the air fryer basket.

- Cook for 10 minutes. Turn halfway through.
- Slice and serve.

Nutrition: Calories 260 Fat 13 g Carbohydrates 1 g Sugar 0 g
Protein 35 g Cholesterol 142 mg

Easy Beef Broccoli

Preparation Time: 10 minutes

Cooking Time: 10 minutes

Servings: 4

Ingredients:

- 1 lb. round beef cubes
- 1/2 medium onion, diced
- 1 tbsp. Worcestershire sauce
- 1/2 lb. broccoli florets, steamed
- 1 tsp. olive oil
- 1 tsp. onion powder
- 1 tsp. garlic powder
- Pepper
- Salt

Directions:

- Spray air fryer basket with cooking spray.

- Add all ingredients except broccoli into the large bowl and toss well.
- Add bowl mixture into the air fryer basket and cook at 360 F for 10 minutes.
- Serve with broccoli and enjoy.

Nutrition: Calories 230 Fat 5 g Carbohydrates 7 g Sugar 3 g Protein 36 g Cholesterol 125 mg

Meatballs

Preparation Time: 10 minutes

Cooking Time: 20 minutes

Servings: 4

Ingredients:

- 1/2 lb. ground beef
- 1/2 lb. Italian sausage
- 1/2 cup cheddar cheese, shredded
- 1/3 tsp. pepper
- 1/2 tsp. garlic powder
- 1 tsp. onion powder

Directions:

- Spray air fryer basket with cooking spray.

- Merge all ingredients into the large bowl and mix until combined.
- Set small balls from meat mixture and place in the air fryer basket.
- Cook at 370 F for 15 minutes. Turn to another side and cook for 5 minutes more.
- Serve and enjoy.

Nutrition: Calories 356 Fat 25 g Carbohydrates 1 g Sugar 0.5 g Protein 32 g Cholesterol 158 mg

Yummy Kabab

Preparation Time: 10 minutes

Cooking Time: 10 minutes

Servings: 4

Ingredients:

- 1 lb. ground beef
- 1/4 cup fresh parsley, chopped
- 1 tbsp. olive oil
- 2 tbsp. kabab spice mix
- 1 tbsp. garlic, minced
- 1 tsp. salt

Directions:s

- Set all ingredients into the bowl and merge until combined. Place in the fridge for 60 minutes.
- Divide meat mixture into four sections and wrap around four soaked wooden skewers.
- Spray air fryer basket with cooking spray.
- Place kabab into the air fryer and cook at 370 F for 10 minutes.
- Serve and enjoy.

Nutrition: Calories 246 Fat 11 g Carbohydrates 1 g Sugar 0.5 g Protein 35 g Cholesterol 125 mg

Broccoli Beef

Preparation Time: 10 minutes

Cooking Time: 12 minutes

Servings: 5

Ingredients:

- 1 lb. round steak, cut into strips
- 1 lb. broccoli florets
- 5 drops liquid stevia
- 1 tsp. soy sauce
- 1/3 cup sherry
- 2 tsp. sesame oil
- 1/3 cup oyster sauce
- 1 garlic clove, minced
- 1 tbsp. ginger, sliced
- 1 tsp. arrowroot powder
- 1 tbsp. olive oil

Directions:

- In a small bowl, merge together oyster sauce, stevia, soy sauce, sherry, arrowroot, and sesame oil.
- Add broccoli and meat in a large bowl.
- Pour oyster sauce mixture over meat and broccoli and toss well. Place in the fridge for 60 minutes.
- Add marinated meat broccoli to the air fryer basket. Drizzle with olive oil and sprinkle with ginger and garlic.

- Cook at 360 F for 12 minutes.
- Serve and enjoy.

Nutrition: Calories 302 Fat 20 g Carbohydrates 8 g Sugar 2 g Protein 24 g Cholesterol 142 mg

Spiced Steak

Preparation Time: 10 minutes

Cooking Time: 9 minutes

Servings: 3

Ingredients:

- 1 lb. rib eye steak
- 1/2 tsp. chipotle powder
- 1/4 tsp. paprika
- 1/4 tsp. onion powder
- 1/2 tsp. garlic powder
- 1 tsp. chili powder
- 1/4 tsp. black pepper
- 1 tsp. coffee powder
- 1/8 tsp. cocoa powder
- 1/8 tsp. coriander powder
- 1 1/2 tsp. sea salt

Directions:

- In a small bowl, merge together all ingredients except steak.
- Rub spice mixture over the steak and let marinate the steak for 20 minutes.
- Spray air fryer basket with cooking spray.
- Preheat the air fryer to 390 F.
- Place marinated steak in the air fryer and cook for 9 minutes.
- Serve and enjoy.

Nutrition: Calories 304 Fat 6 g Carbohydrates 1 g Sugar 0.5 g Protein 54 g Cholesterol 152 mg

Easy Burger Patties

Preparation Time: 10 minutes

Cooking Time: 45 minutes

Servings: 4

Ingredients:

- 10 oz. ground beef
- 1 tsp. dried basil
- 1 tsp. mustard
- 1 tsp. tomato paste
- 1 oz. cheddar cheese
- 1 tsp. mixed herbs
- 1 tsp. garlic puree
- Pepper
- Salt

Directions:s

- Set all ingredients into the large bowl and mix until combined.
- Spray air fryer basket with cooking spray.
- Make patties from meat mixture and place into the air fryer basket.
- Cook at 390 F for 25 minutes then turn patties to another side and cook at 350 F for 20 minutes more.
- Serve and enjoy.

Nutrition:al Value (Amount per Serving): Calories 175 Fat 7 g Carbohydrates 1 g Sugar 2 g Protein 25 g Cholesterol 125 mg

Crisp Pork Chops

Preparation Time: 10 minutes

Cooking Time: 12 minutes

Servings: 6

Ingredients:

- 1 1/2 lbs. pork chops, boneless
- 1 tsp. paprika
- 1 tsp. creole seasoning
- 1 tsp. garlic powder
- 1/4 cup parmesan cheese, grated
- 1/3 cup almond flour

Directions:

- Preheat the air fryer to 360 F.
- Add all ingredients except pork chops in a zip-lock bag.

- Add pork chops in the bag. Seal bag and shake well to coat pork chops.
- Remove pork chops from zip-lock bag and place in the air fryer basket.
- Cook pork chops for 10-12 minutes.
- Serve and enjoy.

Nutrition: Calories 230 Fat 11 g Carbohydrates 2 g Sugar 0.2 g Protein 27 g Cholesterol 79 mg

Parmesan Pork Chops

Preparation Time: 10 minutes

Cooking Time: 15 minutes

Servings: 4

Ingredients:

- 4 pork chops, boneless
- 4 tbsp. parmesan cheese, grated
- 1 cup pork rind
- 2 eggs, lightly beaten
- 1/2 tsp. chili powder
- 1/2 tsp. onion powder
- 1 tsp. paprika
- 1/4 tsp. pepper
- 1/2 tsp. salt

Directions:

- Preheat the air fryer to 400 F.
- Season pork chops with pepper and salt.
- Add pork rind in food processor and process until crumbs form.
- Mix together pork rind crumbs and seasoning in a large bowl.
- Place egg in a separate bowl.
- Dip pork chops in egg mixture then coat with pork crumb mixture and place in the air fryer basket.
- Cook pork chops for 12-15 minutes.
- Serve and enjoy.

Nutrition: Calories 329 Fat 24 g Carbohydrates 1 g Sugar 0.4 g Protein 23 g Cholesterol 158 mg

Meatloaf Sliders

Preparation Time: 10 minutes

Cooking Time: 10 minutes

Servings: 8

Ingredients:

- 1 lb. ground beef
- 1/2 tsp. dried tarragon
- 1 tsp. Italian seasoning
- 1 tbsp. Worcestershire sauce
- 1/4 cup ketchup
- 1/4 cup coconut flour
- 1/2 cup almond flour
- 1 garlic clove, minced
- 1/4 cup onion, chopped
- 2 eggs, lightly beaten
- 1/4 tsp. pepper

- 1/2 tsp. sea salt

Directions:

- Set all ingredients into the mixing bowl and mix until well combined.
- Make the equal shape of patties from mixture and place on a plate. Place in refrigerator for 10 minutes.
- Spray air fryer basket with cooking spray.
- Preheat the air fryer to 360 F.
- Place prepared patties in air fryer basket and cook for 10 minutes.
- Serve and enjoy.

Nutrition: Calories 228 Fat 16 g Carbohydrates 6 g Sugar 2 g Protein 13 g Cholesterol 80 mg

Quick and Easy Steak

Preparation Time: 10 minutes

Cooking Time: 7 minutes

Servings: 2

Ingredients:

- 12 oz. steaks
- 1/2 tbsp. unsweetened cocoa powder
- 1 tbsp. Montreal steak seasoning
- 1 tsp. liquid smoke
- 1 tbsp. soy sauce
- Pepper
- Salt

Directions:

- Add steak, liquid smoke, and soy sauce in a zip-lock bag and shake well.
- Season steak with seasonings and place in the refrigerator for overnight.

- Place marinated steak in air fryer basket and cook at 375 F for 5 minutes.
- Turn steak to another side and cook for 2 minutes more.
- Serve and enjoy.

Nutrition: Calories 356 Fat 8.7 g Carbohydrates 1.4 g Sugar 0.2 g Protein 62.2 g Cholesterol 153 mg

Perfect Cheeseburger

Preparation Time: 5 minutes

Cooking Time: 12 minutes

Servings: 2

Ingredients:

- 1/2 lb. ground beef
- 1/4 tsp. onion powder
- 2 cheese slices
- 1/4 tsp. pepper
- 1/8 tsp. salt

Directions:

- In a bowl, merge together ground beef, onion powder, pepper, and salt.
- Make two equal shapes of patties from meat mixture and place in the air fryer basket.
- Cook patties at 370 F for 12 minutes. Turn patties halfway through.

- Once air fryer timer goes off then place cheese slices on top of each patty and close the air fryer basket for 1 minute.
- Serve and enjoy.

Nutrition: Calories 325 Fat 16.4 g Carbohydrates 0.8 g Sugar 0.3 g Protein 41.4 g Cholesterol 131 mg

Steak Bites with Mushrooms

Preparation Time: 10 minutes

Cooking Time: 18 minutes

Servings: 3

Ingredients:

- 1 lb. steaks, cut into 1/2-inch cubes
- 1/2 tsp. garlic powder
- 1 tsp. Worcestershire sauce
- 2 tbsp. butter, melted
- 8 oz. mushrooms, sliced
- Pepper
- Salt

Directions:

- Set all ingredients into the large mixing bowl and toss well.
- Set air fryer basket with cooking spray.
- Preheat the air fryer to 400 F.
- Add steak mushroom mixture into the air fryer basket and cook at 400 F for 15-18 minutes. Shake basket twice.
- Serve and enjoy.

Nutrition: Calories 388 Fat 15.5 g Carbohydrates 3.2 g Sugar 1.8 g Protein 57.1 g Cholesterol 156 mg

Simple and Tasty Pork Chops

Preparation Time: 10 minutes

Cooking Time: 9 minutes

Servings: 4

Ingredients:

- 4 pork chops, boneless
- 1 tsp. onion powder
- 1 tsp. smoked paprika
- 1/2 cup parmesan cheese, grated
- 2 tbsp. olive oil
- 1/2 tsp. pepper
- 1 tsp. kosher salt

Directions:

- Brush pork chops with olive oil.
- In a bowl, merge together parmesan cheese and spices.
- Spray air fryer basket with cooking spray.

- Coat pork chops with parmesan cheese mixture and place in the air fryer basket.
- Cook pork chops at 375 F for 9 minutes. Turn halfway through.
- Serve and enjoy.

Nutrition: Calories 332   Carbohydrates 1.1 g   Sugar 0.3 g Protein 19.3 g Cholesterol 71 mg

Simple Air Fryer Steak

Preparation Time: 10 minutes

Cooking Time: 18 minutes

Servings: 2

Ingredients:

- 12 oz. steaks, 3/4-inch thick
- 1 tsp. garlic powder
- 1 tsp. olive oil
- Pepper
- Salt

Directions:

- Coat steaks with oil and season with garlic powder, pepper, and salt.

- Preheat the air fryer to 400 F.
- Place steaks in air fryer basket and cook for 15-18 minutes. Turn halfway through.
- Serve and enjoy.

Nutrition: Calories 363   Carbohydrates 1.1 g   Sugar 0.3 g Protein 61.7 g Cholesterol 153 mg

Quick and Tender Pork Chops

Preparation Time: 5 minutes

Cooking Time: 14 minutes

Servings: 3

Ingredients:

- 3 pork chops, rinsed and pat dry
- 1/4 tsp. smoked paprika
- 1/2 tsp. garlic powder
- 2 tsp. olive oil
- Pepper
- Salt

Directions:

- Set pork chops with olive oil and season with paprika, garlic powder, pepper, and salt.

- Place pork chops in air fryer basket and cook at 380 F for 10-14 minutes. Turn halfway through.
- Serve and enjoy.

Nutrition: Calories 285   Carbohydrates 0.5 g   Sugar 0.1 g Protein 18.1 g Cholesterol 69 mg

Pork with Mushrooms

Preparation Time: 10 minutes

Cooking Time: 18 minutes

Servings: 4

Ingredients:

- 1 lb. pork chops, rinsed and pat dry
- 1/2 tsp. garlic powder
- 1 tsp. soy sauce
- 2 tbsp. butter, melted
- 8 oz. mushrooms, halved
- Pepper
- Salt

Directions:

- Preheat the air fryer to 400 F.
- Cut pork chops into the 3/4-inch cubes and place in a large mixing bowl.
- Add remaining ingredients into the bowl and toss well.

- Transfer pork and mushroom mixture into the air fryer basket and cook for 15-18 minutes. Shake basket halfway through.
- Serve and enjoy.

Nutrition: Calories 428   Carbohydrates 2.2 g   Sugar 1.1 g
Protein 27.5 g Cholesterol 113 mg

Quick and Simple Bratwurst with Vegetables

Preparation Time: 10 minutes

Cooking Time: 20 minutes

Servings: 6

Ingredients:

- 1 package bratwurst, sliced 1/2-inch rounds
- 1/2 tbsp. Cajun seasoning
- 1/4 cup onion, diced
- 2 bell pepper, sliced

Directions:s

- Set all ingredients into the mixing bowl and toss well.
- Line air fryer basket with foil.
- Add vegetable and bratwurst mixture into the air fryer basket and cook at 390 F for 10 minutes.
- Toss well and cook for 10 minutes more.
- Serve and enjoy.

Nutrition: Calories 63 Fat 4 g Carbohydrates 4 g Sugar 2 g
Protein 2 g Cholesterol 10 mg

Steak Fajitas Meatloaf Sliders

Preparation Time: 10 minutes
Cooking Time: 15 minutes

Servings: 6

Ingredients:

- 1 lb. steak, sliced
- 1 tbsp. olive oil
- 1 tbsp. fajita seasoning, gluten-free
- 1/2 cup onion, sliced
- 3 bell peppers, sliced

Directions:

- Line air fryer basket with aluminum foil.
- Add all ingredients large bowl and toss until well coated.
- Transfer fajita mixture into the air fryer basket and cook at 390 F for 5 minutes.
- Toss well and cook for 5-10 minutes more.
- Serve and enjoy.

Nutrition: Calories 304 Fat 17 g Carbohydrates 15 g Sugar 4 g Protein 22 g Cholesterol 73 mg

Beef Roast

Preparation Time: 10 minutes

Cooking Time: 35 minutes

Servings: 7

Ingredients:

- 2 lbs. beef roast
- 1 tbsp. olive oil
- 1 tsp. thyme
- 2 tsp. garlic powder
- 1/4 tsp. pepper
- 1 tbsp. kosher salt

Directions:

- Coat roast with olive oil.
- Mix together thyme, garlic powder, pepper, and salt and rub all over roast.
- Place roast into the air fryer basket and cook at 400 F for 20 minutes.

- Spray roast with cooking spray and cook for 15 minutes more.
- Slice and serve.

Nutrition: Calories 238 Fat 13 g Carbohydrates 1 g Sugar 0.5 g Protein 25 g Cholesterol 89 mg

Delicious Cheeseburgers

Preparation Time: 10 minutes

Cooking Time: 12 minutes

Servings: 4

Ingredients:

- 1 lb. ground beef
- 4 cheddar cheese slices
- 1/2 tsp. Italian seasoning
- Pepper
- Salt

Directions:

- Spray air fryer basket with cooking spray.
- In a bowl, mix together ground beef, Italian seasoning, pepper, and salt.
- Make four equal shapes of patties from meat mixture and place into the air fryer basket.

- Cook at 375 F for 5 minutes. Turn patties to another side and cook for 5 minutes more.
- Place cheese slices on top of each patty and cook for 2 minutes more.
- Serve and enjoy.

Nutrition: Calories 325 Fat 16.5 g Carbohydrates 0.4 g Sugar 0.2 g Protein 41.4 g Cholesterol 131 mg

Asian Sirloin Steaks

Preparation Time: 10 minutes

Cooking Time: 20 minutes

Servings: 2

Ingredients:

- 12 oz. sirloin steaks
- 1 tbsp. garlic, minced
- 1 tbsp. ginger, grated
- 1/2 tbsp. Worcestershire sauce
- 1 1/2 tbsp. soy sauce
- 2 tbsp. Erythritol
- Pepper
- Salt

Directions:

- Add steaks in a large zip-lock bag along with remaining ingredients. Shake well and place in the refrigerator for overnight.
- Spray air fryer basket with cooking spray.
- Place marinated steaks in air fryer basket and cook at 400 F for 10 minutes.
- Turn steaks to another side and cook for 10-15 minutes more.
- Serve and enjoy.

Nutrition: Calories 342 Fat 10 g Carbohydrates 5 g Sugar 1 g Protein 52 g Cholesterol 152 mg

Conversion Tables

The unit of measure conversion table is essential in the kitchen when you want to prepare a recipe measured according to a standard different from what you are used to

The recipes are all expressed according to the decimal metric system, but some readers may need to transform them into local measurement systems.

Indeed, some mathematics may be needed initially, but even more, a little logic is necessary because a cup of liquids will weigh differently from a cup of solids, and the same happens with ounces that can measure solid and liquid ingredients.

COOKING CONVERSION CHART

Measurement

CUP	ONCES	MILLILITERS	TABLESPOONS
8 cup	64 oz	1895 ml	128
6 cup	48 oz	1420 ml	96
5 cup	40 oz	1180 ml	80
4 cup	32 oz	960 ml	64
2 cup	16 oz	480 ml	32
1 cup	8 oz	240 ml	16
3/4 cup	6 oz	177 ml	12
2/3 cup	5 oz	158 ml	11
1/2 cup	4 oz	118 ml	8
3/8 cup	3 oz	90 ml	6
1/3 cup	2.5 oz	79 ml	5.5
1/4 cup	2 oz	59 ml	4
1/8 cup	1 oz	30 ml	3
1/16 cup	1/2 oz	15 ml	1

Temperature

FAHRENHEIT	CELSIUS
100 °F	37 °C
150 °F	65 °C
200 °F	93 °C
250 °F	121 °C
300 °F	150 °C
325 °F	160 °C
350 °F	180 °C
375 °F	190 °C
400 °F	200 °C
425 °F	220 °C
450 °F	230 °C
500 °F	260 °C
525 °F	274 °C
550 °F	288 °C

Weight

IMPERIAL	METRIC
1/2 oz	15 g
1 oz	29 g
2 oz	57 g
3 oz	85 g
4 oz	113 g
5 oz	141 g
6 oz	170 g
8 oz	227 g
10 oz	283 g
12 oz	340 g
13 oz	369 g
14 oz	397 g
15 oz	425 g
1 lb	453 g

CPSIA information can be obtained
at www.ICGtesting.com
Printed in the USA
BVHW090334220621
610126BV00012B/2647

9 781803 123493